Dwight Howard

By Jeff Savage

AMAZING ATHLETES

Lerner Publications Company • Minneapolis

Lerner Publications Company
A division of Lerner Publishing Group, Inc.
241 First Avenue North
Minneapolis, MN 55401 U.S.A.

Website address: www.lernerbooks.com

Library of Congress Cataloging-in-Publication Data

Savage, Jeff, 1961–
        Dwight Howard / by Jeff Savage.
            p.   cm. — (Amazing athletes)
        Includes bibliographical references and index.
        ISBN: 978–0–7613–5748–3 (lib. bdg. : alk. paper)
        1. Howard, Dwight—Juvenile literature. 2. Basketball players—United States—Biography—
    Juvenile literature. I. Title.
    GV884.H68S26 2011
    796.323092—dc22 [B]   2009039364

Manufactured in the United States of America
1 – BP – 7/15/10

TABLE OF CONTENTS

Dwight Howard *(right)* takes a shot against the Cleveland Cavaliers in Game 6 of the 2009 Eastern Conference Finals.

A MAGIC SHOW

Dwight Howard, **center** for the Orlando Magic, called for the basketball. Anthony Johnson passed it to him near the basket. Two Cleveland Cavaliers pressed up against Dwight. He rose up and gently flicked a **hook shot** over the defenders. Swish!

Dwight's team was leading 44–32 in Game 6 of the 2009 Eastern Conference Finals. With a victory, the Magic would reach the National Basketball Association (NBA) Finals for the first time in 14 years. Dwight was dominating the Cavaliers again, just as he had the whole series. Cleveland tried everything against Orlando's 6-foot-11, 270-pound big man. But even with LeBron James, the league's Most Valuable Player, (MVP) on its team, the Cavaliers could not stop Dwight.

Dwight *(left)* shoots against Zydrunas Ilgauskas.

When Dwight touched the ball next, three defenders surrounded him. Dwight whipped a pass to Rashard Lewis behind the three-point line. Lewis buried the long **jump shot**. After a Cavs miss, the Magic rushed back down the court. Johnson bounced a pass down low. Dwight gathered it in with his soft hands. Then he slammed down a thunderous **dunk**! The 17,461 fans at Amway Arena in Florida leaped from their seats. Dwight did not flex his muscles or beat his chest, as some players do after a dunk. Instead, he simply smiled and ran back to play defense. "I'm going to laugh, because it's fun," Dwight says. "Some people want to see a mean streak, but that's justnot me."

Dwight smiles during the Eastern Conference Finals.

The colors of Dwight's uniform—black and blue—fit his bruising style. That's why he was voted the NBA's 2009 Defensive Player of the Year. But when a game ends, you can find him in his team's locker room or joking with his teammates.

The Magic defeated the Cavaliers, 103–90. Dwight scored 40 points. The Magic would face the Los Angeles Lakers in the NBA Finals. In the locker room, Dwight told reporters, "We can beat anybody." He said it with a smile.

Dwight grew up in Swainsboro, Georgia *(above)*.

THE MIRACLE CHILD

Dwight David Howard was born December 8, 1985, in Atlanta, Georgia. He grew up in the nearby town of Swainsboro. His father, Dwight Sr., is a police officer. His mother, Sheryl, played on the women's basketball team at Morris Brown College. Sheryl lost seven children to miscarriage before Dwight was born. Dwight's parents call him the Miracle Child. Dwight still thinks hard about that. "My dad always told me that I was a blessing." Dwight now has a sister, TaShanda, and a brother, Jahaziel.

Dwight's parents taught him discipline and character. Dwight used these traits in the classroom—and on the basketball court. He played hard while laughing and praising his teammates. His father was his coach for several seasons in local leagues. "Stop smiling out there!" his father would shout. Dwight would tell his dad he was thrilled to be playing. By 1996, Dwight was competing against eighth graders. "They were smarter and stronger," he said, "So I learned."

Dwight learned to dribble and pass by playing **point guard**. He is left-handed, but in 2000 he suffered a broken wrist. After that, he was forced to shoot with his right hand. He became great using either hand. In 2001, his first year at Southwest Atlanta Christian Academy, Dwight grew six inches to reach 6 foot 9. He switched to **forward**. That year, he wrote a list of goals for life. Among them was leading his high school team to a state title. He also wanted to be the first overall pick in the NBA **draft**.

Dwight had other interests as a young adult. He sang in the school choir. He was a pitcher for

Dwight's favorite movie is *Finding Nemo*. His favorite character is Dory. "She's silly and makes me laugh," he says. "I love kids' movies because I'm a big kid."

the school's baseball team. He went bowling every Monday night with friends. He was even voted class president. "I was always trying to make people laugh," Dwight said. "I might have been the silliest person ever." Dwight's first love was basketball. High school teammate Austin Dudley said, "When the rest of us would go off to the movies, Dwight would be in the gym practicing."

Dwight played basketball in high school for Southwest Atlanta Christian Academy.

Dwight drives to the basket
in high school.

TOP PICK

Dwight was the best team player. He cared
about winning, not his own statistics. "He
looked out for me and everybody else," said

Austin Dudley. "To him, everybody was equal." Southwest Atlanta Christian Academy won with teamwork. In 2003, Dwight's third year, the team finished with a 30–3 record. The school reached the state championship game before losing.

As a **senior**, Dwight took his team one step further. He averaged 25 points, 18 **rebounds**, and eight **blocks** for the season. In the state title game, he had 26 points, 23 rebounds, and 10 blocks. Dwight and his teammates won the game and became state champions. He was named Mr. Basketball in the state of Georgia and was widely considered the nation's best high school player.

The question was not whether an NBA team would draft Dwight. The question was how soon.

Some experts said Dwight would be the first player chosen in the 2004 draft. The Orlando Magic got first pick. Their choice was easy. They picked Dwight. "I was hoping for a magical moment," he said.

As an 18-year-old **rookie**, Dwight showed such promise that he was named the starting center for the Magic. Playing against NBA superstars was a huge leap from high school. Facing San Antonio Spurs great Tim Duncan for the first time, Dwight turned and took a shot. The ball went over the backboard. "I was so

Dwight's name is written on the draft board next to the Magic.

NBA DRAFT

NBA DR
1st Ro

TEAM	PLAYER	POS
ORLANDO MAGIC	Dwight Howard	
CHARLOTTE BOBCATS		
CHICAGO BULLS		
LOS ANGELES CLIPPERS		

Dwight *(center)* is presented with a Magic jersey by team officials after being named the first pick in the draft.

amazed that I was playing against Tim Duncan that I got scared," Dwight admitted. "The game looks so easy when I watch it on film. But when I'm out there in front of 20,000 fans, it's a different feeling."

Magic coach Johnny Davis said, "In high school Dwight could just turn around and shoot over guys. Now he's gone from the kiddie pool to the adult pool."

Dwight plays defense alongside Magic veteran Grant Hill *(arms raised)*.

PUTTING IN THE WORK

The Magic took care of Dwight. The team had a personal chef prepare his meals. A personal **trainer** led his strength training. Soon Dwight was the strongest player on the team. His

locker was next to **veteran** Grant Hill. The team wanted Dwight to learn from Hill.

Dwight wound up starting all 82 games of the season. He became the first NBA player directly out of high school to do so. In his first game against the Milwaukee Bucks, Dwight scored 12 points and grabbed 10 rebounds. The performance was no fluke. Those numbers—12 and 10—turned out to be Dwight's average for the season.

Dwight takes the ball to the basket during a game in 2004, his rookie season.

Dwight admits he is highly competitive. "I once practiced a whole year to beat my cousin in this one [video] game," he says. "When he came home for the summer, I couldn't beat him. I got so mad I threw the controller out the window."

Dwight often praised his teammates. "Everybody loves him," teammate Tony Battie said. "He's our shining star." But the Magic lost most of their games. Dwight was unfamiliar with losing. "I tried to be the last one in the shower so my teammates wouldn't see me crying," he said.

NBA Hall of Fame center Patrick Ewing joined the Magic coaching staff for the 2005–2006 season. "What kind of player do you want to be?" Ewing asked Dwight. "The greatest," Dwight replied. Ewing grinned. "Then you have to put in the work," he said. Dwight

Dwight talks with Magic assistant coach Patrick Ewing.

had received the very same advice from Hall of Famer Michael Jordan. Dwight took their advice seriously.

Dwight worked harder than ever. He ate smartly, lifted weights, and gained 20 pounds of muscle. He practiced several hours a day on his moves near the basket and on his defense. Around the net, he grabbed the ball often. He became the youngest player in history to lead the NBA in total rebounds. But the Magic missed the **playoffs** again.

Dwight kept pushing. He worked harder. In the 2006–2007 season, he played in all 82

Dwight practices free throws.

Dwight pulls down a rebound while playing against the Detroit Pistons in 2006.

games for the third straight year. He scored a career-high 32 points against the Toronto Raptors. Later, he scored 35 against the Philadelphia 76ers. "He's a freak of nature," said superstar Kevin Garnett. Dwight led the league in total rebounds again and was ninth in blocks. And finally, the Magic got to the playoffs. They lost to the Detroit Pistons in the first round, but it was a step forward.

Dwight signed a huge contract with the Magic in 2007.

SUPERMAN

The Magic knew their future depended on Dwight. They gave him a new five-year **contract** for $80 million. Dwight did not act rich. Instead, he kept his boyhood charm.

He teased new coach Stan Van Gundy and other NBA players. He played pranks, like going to movie theaters wearing a mask to scare the audience. "I like to see people jump," he said. At hotels during road trips, he and teammate Jameer Nelson pounded on doors and ran down the hall. "He's going to make you have fun," said Nelson. "When you see Dwight, you're going to have a good day."

Dwight jokes with the media at a news conference.

On the court, Dwight dominated more than ever. In one game against the Golden State Warriors, he grabbed more rebounds than the entire Warriors starting lineup. Along the way, he earned the nickname Superman. "But at the end of 'Superman' is 'man.' I'm still human," said Dwight. "I don't fly to the moon at night. I sleep in a bed, see the same stars, and breathe the same air."

Dwight goes for a bucket while playing against the Golden State Warriors.

Dwight wears a Superman costume as he soars toward the basket during the 2008 Slam Dunk Contest.

Fans voted Dwight a starter for the 2008 NBA All-Star Game. He wore a Superman cape to win the Slam Dunk Contest. That season, he became the league's youngest rebounding champion ever. The Magic made the playoffs again—and won! They beat the Toronto Raptors in the first round before losing to Detroit again. "It hurt so bad losing to them again," said Dwight, "that I didn't want anything to do with basketball for a couple weeks."

Dwight happily played as the starting center for the United States at the 2008 Olympic Games. Team USA won all of its games in Beijing, China, to capture the gold medal.

Dwight was wildly popular. For the 2009 NBA All-Star Game, he received over three million votes, the most by any player ever.

Dwight *(second from left)* holds up his gold medal after the final game at the 2008 Olympics in Beijing.

Orlando rolled through the playoffs in 2009. The team beat the 76ers, the defending champion Boston Celtics, and finally the Cavaliers. The Magic lost in the title round to the Lakers.

Dwight has already achieved some of his goals, like appearing in commericals and acting in movies.

Everything about Dwight is big—his body, his dreams, even his house! It has six fireplaces, several flat-screen TVs, and a game room. On the ceiling above his bed is a list of goals.

But if you met Dwight, you'd never guess he was a rich superstar. "I'm real proud of myself for not letting the things of the world—the money, the fame—get to me," he says. "I think about how all this can be taken away."

"What inspires me are . . . all the little kids who dream of making it to the NBA," Dwight says. "I had that dream . . . and never let anybody take it away. My motto was always, 'Never let anybody tell me I can't do anything.'"

Dwight is more than just thankful. He is a giver. He has traveled to Africa to help plant food gardens. He has built a house for Habitat for Humanity. He has visited sick children in hospitals, calling himself Dr. Giggles. To many, he is a real Superman. "There is a superhero in everyone," says Dwight. "I ask my friends, 'If you had one power, what would it be?' They wish they could fly or see into the future. I've always wanted to touch peoples' lives. I want the ability to make everybody's life better."

Selected Career Highlights

2008–2009
Named NBA Defensive Player of the Year
Led Orlando Magic to NBA Finals
Leading vote-getter for NBA All-Star Team
Named to All-NBA First Team
Led NBA in total rebounds and rebounds per game
Led NBA in dunks

2007–2008
Won NBA Slam Dunk Contest
Starting center for Team USA at Olympic Games
Won Olympic Gold Medal
Voted to second NBA All-Star Game
Named to All-NBA First Team
Led NBA in total rebounds and rebounds per game

2006–2007
Voted to first NBA All-Star Game
Led NBA in total rebounds
Finished second in NBA in rebounds per game
Named to All-NBA Third Team

2005–2006
Led NBA in total rebounds
Finished second in NBA in rebounds per game

2004–2005
Unanimous selection to NBA All-Rookie First Team
Finished third in voting for NBA Rookie of the Year

2003–2004
Led Southwest Atlanta Christian Academy to state
   championship title
Named Naismith Player of the Year
Named Gatorade National Player of the Year
Named McDonald's National High School Player
   of the Year
Named Morgan Wootten High School Player
   of the Year
Named co-MVP of McDonald's High School
   All-American Game

2003
Led Southwest Atlanta Christian Academy to state
   championship game

Glossary

blocks: stopping shots from going to the hoop by striking the ball

center: a player on a basketball team who usually plays close to the basket

contract: a written deal signed by a player and a team

draft: a yearly event in which professional teams take turns choosing new players from a selected group

dunk: a shot in which the player slams the ball forcefully through the basket

forward: a player on a basketball team who usually plays close to the basket. Forwards need to rebound and shoot the ball well.

hook shot: a shot, usually attempted near the basket, in which the shooter is sideways to the basket while shooting with one hand

jump shot: a shot in which the player jumps in the air and releases the ball at a distance from the basket

playoffs: a series of games to decide the league's champion

point guard: the player on a basketball team who is responsible for running the team's offensive plays. Point guards are skilled at dribbling and passing the ball.

rebounds: grabs of missed shots from near the hoop

rookie: a first-year player

senior: fourth year of high school or college

trainer: a fitness expert who teaches a person exercises and proper nutrition

veteran: a player with two or more years of experience

Further Reading & Websites

Basen, Ryan. *Dwight Howard: Gifted and Giving Basketball Star*. Berkeley Heights, NJ: Enslow Publishers, 2010.

Harasymiw, Malcolm J. *Dwight Howard: Emerging Basketball Superstar*. New York: Gareth Stevens Publishing, 2010.

Kennedy, Mike, and Mark Stewart. *Swish: The Quest for Basketball's Perfect Shot*. Minneapolis: Millbrook Press, 2009.

Savage, Jeff. *LeBron James*. Minneapolis: Lerner Publications Company, 2006.

Dwight's Website
http://www.dwighthoward.com
Dwight's official website, featuring news, records, photos, trivia, and other information about Dwight and his team.

Official NBA Site
http://www.nba.com
The official National Basketball Association website that provides fans with game results, statistics, schedules, and biographies of players.

Sports Illustrated Kids
http://www.sikids.com
The *Sports Illustrated Kids* website covers all sports, including basketball.

Index

Photo Acknowledgments

The images in this book are used with the permission of: AP Photo/
Chris O'Meara, pp. 4, 5; AP Photo/Reinhold Matay, p. 7; Jerry Cadle/City of
Swainsboro, p. 8; AP Photo/John Amis, p. 11; AP Photo/Nick Wass, p. 12; AP
Photo/Peter Cosgrove, pp. 14, 15, 17; AP Photo/Pat Sullivan, p. 16; AP Photo/
David Zalubowski, p. 19; AP Photo/John Raoux, pp. 20, 21, 23; AP Photo/Jeff
Chiu, p. 22; AP Photo/Marcio Jose Sanchez, p. 24; AP Photo/Eric Gay, pp. 25,
26; AP Photo/Scott Audetter, Pool, p. 29.

Front Cover: AP Photo/Matt York